DISCOVER BY COLORING

INSECTS

REPTILES

MAMMALS

BIRDS

DINOSAURS

Discovering Insects

What is...?

What is...?

What is...?

What is...?

What is...?

What is...?

What is...?

What is...?

What is...?

What is...?

The insects' party

Discovering birds

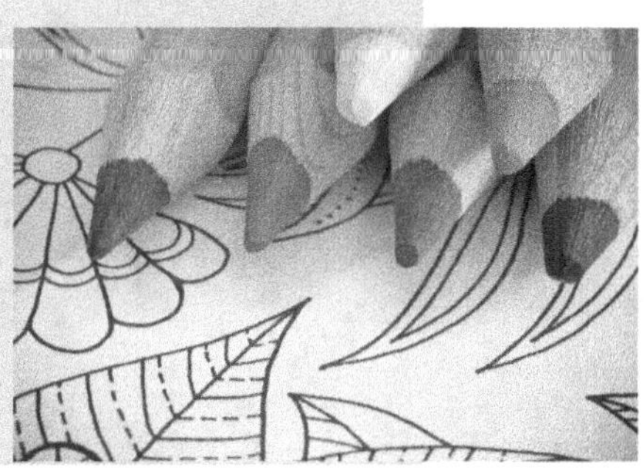

What is....?

What is....?

What is...?

What is...?

What is...?

What is...?

What is...?

What is...?

What is...?

What is...?

What is...?

What is...?

What is...?

IN THE WOODS...

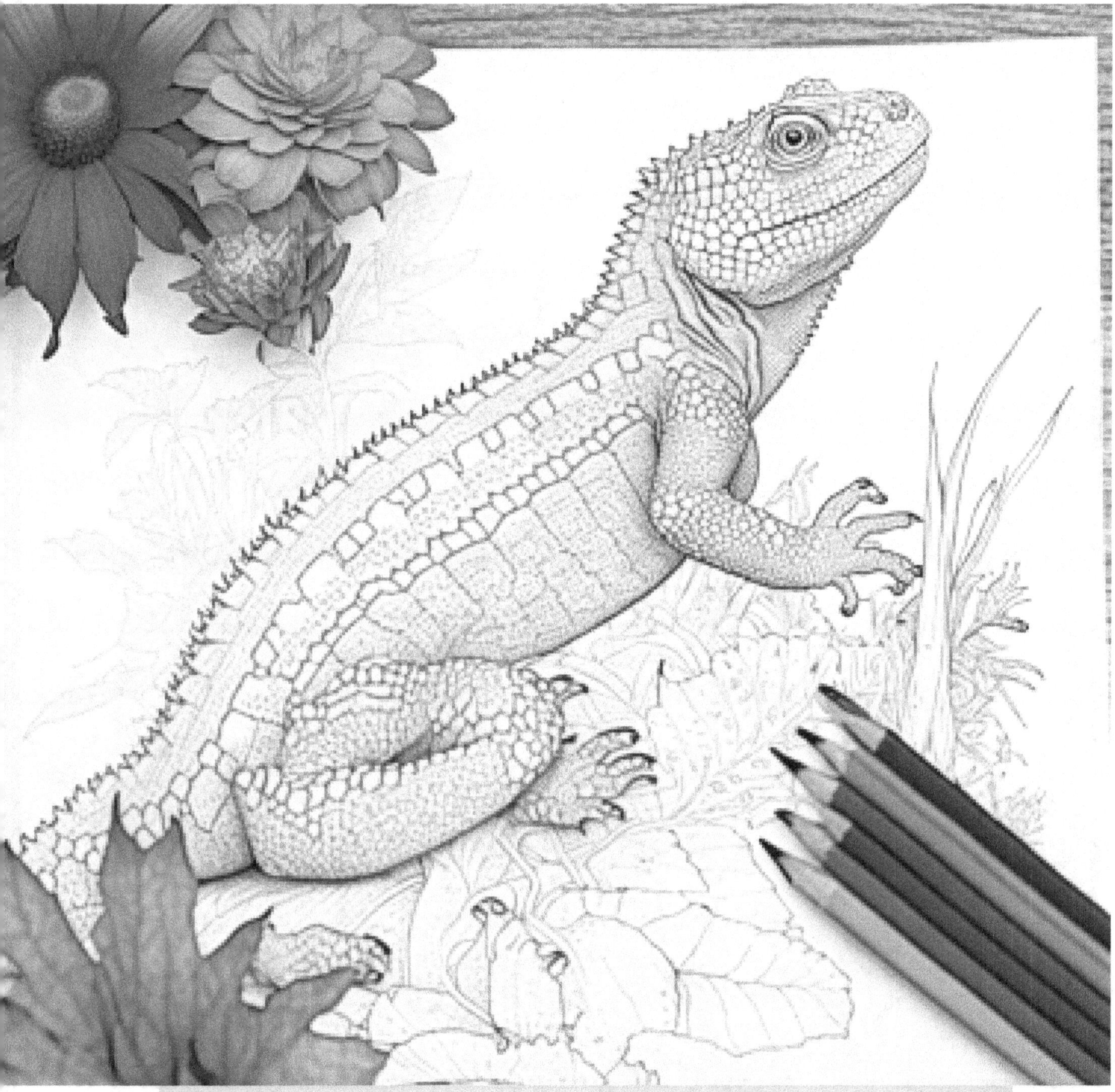

Discovering the reptiles

What is...?

What is....?

**What is...?

What is...?

What is...?

What is...?

What is...?

What is...?

What is...?

What is...?

CELEBRATING

Discovering
Mammals

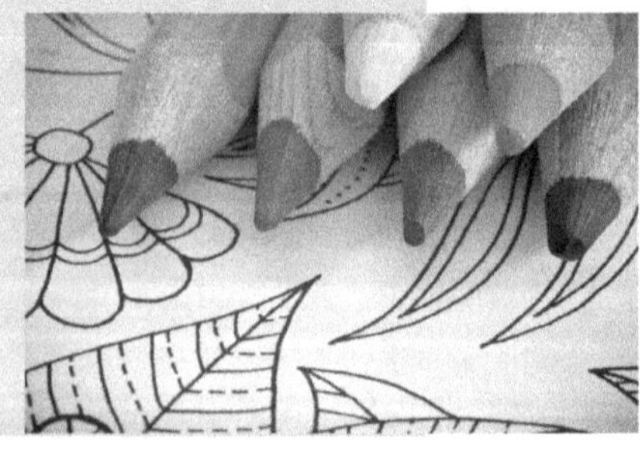

What is....?

What is...?

What is...?

What is...?

What is...?

What is...?

What is...?

What is...?

What is....?

What is...?

What is...?

What is...?

What is...?

PLAYING

FICTITIOUS AND MYTHOLOGICAL ANIMALS

What is....?

What is....?

**What is...?

What is...?

What is....?

**What is...?

What is...?

What is...?

What is....?

What is...?

Extra images

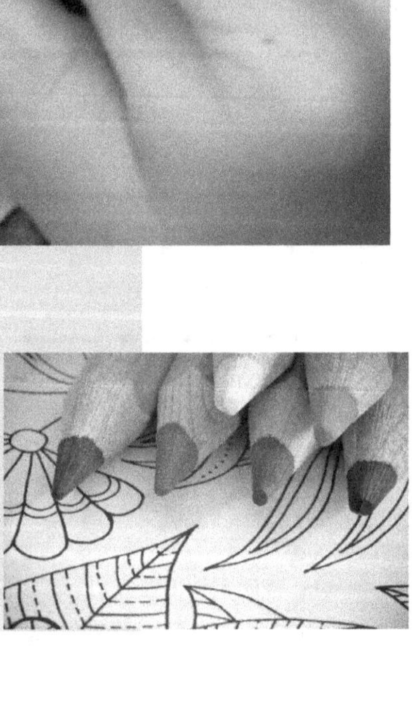

What is....?

What is...?

What is...?

What is...?

What is...?

What is....?